INJURY-FREE RUNNING

RUNNER'S WORLD BEST

INJURY-FREE RUNNING

Edited by Adam Bean and the editors of
Runner's World® Magazine

RODALE

First published in 2006 by Rodale International Ltd., London, England
© 2006 by Rodale Inc.

Interior photographs: Brand X Pictures, 23; Corbis, 3; IndexOpen/Ablestock, 85; IndexOpen/Keith Levit Photography, 91; IndexOpen/LLC, FogStock, 55; IndexOpen/Peter Adams, 92; istockphoto/Eliza Snow, 83; istockphoto/Mark Pierce, 51; istockphoto/Oleg Prikhodko, 6; Jupiter Images, 13, 21, 66, 69, 71, 75, 81, 87; Michael Mazzeo, 25, 26, 27, 28, 29, 30, 31, 33, 34, 35, 36, 37, 38, 39, 41, 42, 43, 44, 45, 46, 47, 48, 49, 50; Photodisc, 58; Pixtal, 16; Primal Images, 63, 67, 72; Rodale Picture Library, 64, 84; Shutterstock/Carolina, 77; Shutterstock/Galina Barskaya, 19, 52; Shutterstock/Karen Roach, 10; Shutterstock/Ljupco Smokovski, 61; Shutterstock/Mrs Gill Martin, 79; Shutterstock/Simone van den Berg, 9; Shutterstock/Soundsnaps, 89; Shutterstock/Winthrop Brookhouse, 14

Runner's World ® is a registered trademark of Rodale Inc.

Printed and bound in the U.K. by CPI Bath using acid-free paper from sustainable resources

Library of Congress Catalog-in-Publication data is on file with the publisher.

ISBN-10 1–59486–375–X
ISBN-13 978–1–59486–375–2

Distributed to the trade by Holtzbrinck Publishers

1   3   5   7   9   8   6   4   2

Also available: *Runner's World Best: Getting Started, Runner's World Best: Run Faster*

We inspire and enable people to improve their lives and the world around them

CONTENTS

Introduction

Educating yourself on the various injuries associated with running can help you avoid them.

Part of the beauty of running is that it doesn't require special skills. It's open to the young and old, to the trim and the not-so-trim. It knows no socioeconomic bounds; it favors no religions, races, or creeds. Beginning and out-of-shape runners can experience joys and pains similar to those the world's elite racers experience.

Trying to stretch your limits—whether it's learning to jog a mile around your neighborhood or pushing yourself to shave a few seconds off your 100-meter time—can result in some aches and pains, of course. And sometimes injury occurs.

But the good news is that you can prevent most of those injuries. "An ounce of prevention is worth a pound of cure" are words to live by. And if you do get injured, with the right treatment you can be back on the road, trail or track in a relatively short period of time.

But you need to know what to look for and how to respond. And that's what *Injury-Free Running* will help you do. Through this book, you will learn to

Prevent injuries from happening. The best way to beat injuries is to understand them. For each injury you will be supplied with steps you can take to help avoid them. From stretches to equipment choices to training tips, you'll have all the knowledge you need to steer clear of the pitfalls.

Recognize the early symptoms. At the first twinge of discomfort many runners simply decide to tough it out and run through the pain. This is not a good idea. Read about the early telltale signs of running injuries so that you won't end up further aggravating them.

Respond to those symptoms. After you identify an injury you must insure you receive the proper treatment. Whether you visit a doctor or treat yourself, you'll be given the proper guidance to make sure your particular ailment receives the appropriate care.

Recover smartly and efficiently. We all want to recover from our injuries as quickly as possible, but rushing back too fast can cause major setbacks and the risk of more severe damage. Find out about the recovery timetables for specific injuries and alternative ways to maintain your fitness level while you're on the mend.

In Part I you'll learn about warming up, basic training principles, how to avoid overuse injuries, how to identify your specific type of gait and select the right running shoes—and how to know when it's time to replace those shoes. In short, you'll be given a practical primer on the fundamentals of injury prevention.

Part II includes flexibility and strength training programs, all with photos and clear step-by-step descriptions, to help you stay injury-free. You'll learn how to stay flexible, supple, and strong—and become a stronger, faster runner at the same time.

In Part III you'll learn about injuries that occur to runners, from heatstroke to frostbite, from runner's knee to Achilles tendonitis, and more. For each injury, you'll learn how to recognize its symptoms, how to treat it, what to expect during recovery and how to prevent the injury from happening in the first place.

Because sometimes things do go wrong, Part IV covers how to cope with injury, not only physically but also mentally, and how—if you have to take time off your running routine—you can come back in great condition. Young or old, fast or slow, racer or fitness runner, you can use this book to guide you down the path you most want to be on: your favorite running path, running injury-free and easy.

DEBUNKING RUNNING MYTHS

Myths abound in running. If you believed them all, you'd have to pluck up courage just to lace up your shoes. Here is a sampling of running injury myths—and the truth about them.

Myth: You should run through pain.

Fact: No! A mild pain can easily become something major. You need to stop, find out the cause of the problem and fix it.

Myth: To become a better runner, you need to pile on the mileage.

Fact: Dramatically increasing your mileage usually leads to injury, lingering fatigue or mental burnout. The best way to improve is to increase the length of your long run by 1–2 miles (1.6–3.2 km) every two to three weeks.

Myth: Running faster gives you more satisfaction.

Fact: Many runners say that almost all of their running satisfaction comes from covering the distance, crossing the finish line and enjoying the camaraderie of fellow runners. Don't let your goal stop you from enjoying the pursuit.

Myth: If you run a marathon, you should run every step of it.

Fact: Unless you're aiming for a 2:10 finish, there is no benefit in running continuously. Walking early and regularly during long training runs and races helps conserve energy and can result in faster times.

Myth: Lengthen your stride to run faster and easier.

Fact: Distance runners tend to naturally shorten their stride slightly as they improve their speed and endurance. The key to easier running is keeping your feet low to the ground, with a stride length that doesn't produce a "braking" action or tension in the leg muscles. Running like this increases speed and efficiency.

PART I:
INJURY
PREVENTION

The Warm-Up Controversy

Debates are common about the value of warming up before running, and specifically about stretching before running. Studies agree, however, that stretching after running can help increase flexibility and reduce muscle soreness. And the consensus from most experienced runners is that warming up before running—and cooling down afterward—does help avoid injuries.

A proper cool-down routine after a run is every bit as important as your warm-up.

When you get up in the morning, your muscles and soft tissues are tight. In fact, your muscles are generally about 10 percent shorter than normal. As you start moving around, they stretch to their normal resting length. And when you start to exercise the muscles, they stretch to about 10 percent more than normal resting length—which means that from the time you get out of bed until the muscle is warmed up, it stretches as much as 20 percent. Simply put, a longer muscle is much less likely to become injured than a short, tight muscle, because it can exert more force with less effort.

Failing to cool down can be even more disastrous. Many runners try to get the most out of their runs by sprinting the last couple hundred yards or so, and then just stop. This is asking for injury.

Almost all exercise-related heart attacks occur just after runners stop running. When you exercise, your muscles help pump the blood from your legs to your heart and brain. When you stop running, that muscle action stops and your heart and brain suddenly get less blood and oxygen. Cooling down, however, helps keep the blood flowing to the muscles and allows your body to work its way down from a state of high exertion to the eventual resting condition.

So what's our advice?

Warm up in the traditional way of slow jogging, by doing some gentle stretches if that prepares you the best for your run. Listen to your body. Start your run slowly and pick up the pace as you loosen up.

Cool down afterward by walking for at least a few minutes and then stretching. This removes lactic acid and other waste products from your muscle tissue and helps reduce muscle soreness.

MENTAL WARM-UPS

Along with light running and stretching, many runners also prepare themselves mentally before each run. Having your mind in synch with your body is always a good idea. Two popular mental warm-ups runners use are visualization and verbal affirmation.

Visualization: The act of visualizing yourself running with ease and perfect form prior to going out and doing it, has been scientifically proven to affect your body's response. As peculiar as it may sound, your muscles can be trained to perform as you imagine them to.

Verbal affirmation: Conducting a positive internal dialogue is another way to psych yourself up before a run. Telling yourself things like "I really feel strong today" and "I'm sure I can run farther than usual today" will resonate with you as you hit the road.

Train with Your Brain

More injuries are caused by improper training than from anything else—training too little, training too much, and failing to cross train by working out in other sports. These eleven tips will help you steer clear of injury and keep your regimen running smoothly.

IDENTIFY YOUR GOALS

Build your training around your goals. Do you just want to improve your general fitness? Are you a beginner who would like to run five-kilometer races? Are you looking to advance to half-marathons, marathons, or ultramarathons? Are you a serious racer looking to shave time off your track and road race performances? Once you identify your goals, you can design a training plan.

HAVE A PLAN

If your training is on autopilot, sooner or later you're bound to crash. Design a training plan with your goals in mind. Plan how many miles you will log weekly and monthly, and what types of training you will incorporate (speed workouts, hill running, intervals, weight training).

Here are some plan basics: Increase weekly training mileage by no more than 10 percent per week; plan at least one easy day after every hard day of training or racing; if you're a beginner, don't schedule any hard workouts until you've built up stamina and strength; change only one part of your training at a time (never increase both weekly distance and speed). Finally, allow flexibility depending on your schedule, your progress, and pains or injuries that may occur.

KEEP A DIARY

A training diary helps you see how you're progressing toward your goals and helps you identify areas that need improvement, such as speed work or strength training. It can also be a great motivational tool and can help you avoid injury. You can see what training or conditions precipitated aches and pains, and alter your program where needed.

You can buy a training diary or create your own, in a simple notebook or on a computer calendar program. (See the sample diary on page 92.) Log what you find most useful. Avoid extraneous details, and note only what is helpful to remember: mileage, time, exertion level, and extreme weather conditions. Track your effort levels, as well, by noting next to your times whether it was a hard effort or an easy run. Check your heart rate each morning before you arise and note it. To do this, use your fingers to count your heartbeats in 10 seconds, at your wrist, and multiply that number by six.

TOO MUCH TOO SOON

Your running is going great, and you're eager to increase your speed or your mileage. But doing too much too soon can backfire. You can burn out physically, and mentally, and running may start to seem like a chore rather than something you look forward to. And you risk injuring yourself by pushing too hard before your muscles and tendons are capable of handling the stress of training.

Follow the *10 percent rule* (never increase weekly mileage more than 10 percent); never try to increase both speed and distance at the same time. Never go for long runs two days in a row or run fast two days in a row. Don't run long one day and fast the next—you'll be stressing weakened tissues your body is trying to repair. Beginners should mix running and walking until the body adapts.

It's better to log mileage you can handle week after week than to cram in a month of eye-popping

Keeping a training diary is a great way to monitor your progress.

(and perhaps hamstring-popping) training that leaves you burned out or injured—or both.

LISTEN TO YOUR BODY

If there is a mantra to this book, it is this: *Listen to your body.* If you don't pay attention to your body, minor aches and pains become minor injuries, and minor injuries can become major ones.

Running on softer surfaces can help ease the impact on your joints.

Your body talks to you all the time. That tightness in your right calf may be telling you to stretch the muscles. That ache in your upper back may be telling you your running form is out of whack. That stress in your facial, neck, or arm muscles is telling you that you need to make adjustments to your pace, your form, or both. That twinge in your Achilles heel is whispering a warning to you. The lethargy you feel may be your body telling you it's time to take a day off.

Pay attention to those whispers and warnings before they become a shout or an "I-told-you-so."

DON'T OVERTRAIN

Goals are great. But if you aim recklessly at them, determined to reach them no matter what your body is telling you, you slip into overtraining—doing more than your body or mind can handle.

Signs of overtraining include increased fatigue, sleep disturbances, reduced concentration, apathy, irritability, depression, decreased performance, and delayed recovery. You may have a higher resting heart rate, poor appetite and a depressed immune system (which makes you susceptible to colds and other ailments). Menstrual periods may stop in women.

The remedy is simple: cut back. Use your training diary to help determine a healthier level of training. Add more rest days. During your runs, you should be able to talk in complete sentences (not, of course, during hard runs, speed work, or races).

GETTING THE MOST FROM YOUR RUNNING SHOES

Want to squeeze just a few more miles from that pair of running shoes? The fact is you're asking for injury by running in worn-out shoes. And your shoes may need replacing long before you realize. While the outside may not show much wear, the parts of your shoe that absorb the pounding of running are what wears out.

As a general rule of thumb, replace your running shoes every 500 miles (805 km). But they can wear out faster or last longer, depending on the shoe, your running efficiency, and the surfaces on which you run. Here are a few tricks to help determine when your shoes need replacing:

• Stick your finger into the midsole, inside the shoe, to see if it feels brittle or compressed.

• With one hand inside your shoe and one on the sole, compare the cushioning under the big toe area (one of the most stressed) to other areas. Move the heel counter from side to side with your hands—if it moves too easily or makes a noise, it may be shot.

• Set your shoes on a table and check to see if they tilt to one side or the other.

• Listen to your aches and pains—they are often a sign that you need to buy new shoes.

To extend the life of your shoes and help protect yourself from injury, buy a new pair and alternate wearing them and your current pair. Alternating shoes lets you compare how they feel and makes you more aware of your old ones becoming too flexible or losing their cushioning. It also lets the shoes decompress and dry out thoroughly between uses.

Wash your shoes by hand, with a mild soap and a soft brush as needed. Never put them in a washing machine or dryer. Also, because sunlight and cold can speed up shoe breakdown, store them in a cool, dry place in the summer, and in warmer spaces during the winter.

TRAIN WISELY

Mix cross training into your program, such as running on Mondays, Wednesdays, and Fridays and cycling or swimming on Tuesdays,

Thursdays, and Saturdays. Schedule strength training, and don't neglect your stretching program.

Cross training helps prevent overuse injuries, and can also help you gain strength and flexibility. The activities that best mimic running without its stresses include running in a pool, using an elliptical trainer at the gym, cycling, and inline skating. But you'll also benefit from swimming, rowing, cross-country skiing, yoga, and strength training. The possibilities are substantial, and the benefits are real.

CHOOSE WISELY

Running with someone can be a great boost to your training and can make workouts more pleasurable. But choose companions who have goals and training plans that are compatible with yours. If you train at a 6:00-minute pace and your friend is pushing to maintain a 7:30 pace, you'll both be frustrated, and the slower runner risks injury by trying to keep up. But realize that once in a while, you can slow down and enjoy a slower run with a friend—and still benefit from it.

Cross-training activities such as cycling are the perfect complement to your running routine.

TRAIN TO RACE

Your running needs to resemble the event you're training for. If you want to run 6:30 per mile in your next 10-K (6.2 mi) run, you need to do some training at that pace. Of course you don't train the entire race distance at that pace, but you need to get your body used to the speed you want to run.

Keep your racing within bounds of your training. It's fine to use races as training runs, but keep your racing within reason and, just as with your training, don't do too much racing too

STEER CLEAR OF OVERUSE INJURIES

An overuse injury occurs slowly, over time—not from a single traumatic incident. The good news is that if you heed early warning signs, you can avoid many injuries and greatly speed recovery time for ones that do occur.

Overuse injuries are caused by one of four factors:

1. **Inadequate recovery**—you're not letting your body fully recover from one run to the next. You can help solve this problem by paying attention to your body and by consulting your training diary to figure out where problems occur (and by following the simple rule of taking at least one easy day after a hard day).

2. **Biomechanical irregularities**—our bodies aren't perfect, and it isn't uncommon to have one leg longer than the other or to turn your ankle excessively when you run. The right shoes can help and a podiatrist or physical therapist may prescribe lifts or orthotics— shoe inserts that help correct any possible irregularities.

3. **Muscular imbalances**—these may include having quadriceps that are stronger than hamstrings, which can cause hamstring or knee problems. To solve imbalances, follow a stretching and strengthening routine designed just for runners (see Part II, beginning on page 23).

4. **Improper footwear**—inadequate shoes can exacerbate all the above problems. This section explains how to select the right shoes (see pages 19–21) and how to recognize when it's time for a new pair (see page 15).

soon. Build up, prepare, and know your race pace. By all means, test and push yourself, but within reason. Don't push yourself to unreasonable limits.

CHOOSE THE RIGHT SHOE

Shoes can make—or break—a runner. Every mile you run, your feet absorb roughly 110 tons of energy. With every stride, your foot and leg absorb a force more than three times your body weight. Your shoes act as shock absorbers, cushioning that impact and distributing that force.

You're asking for trouble if you're running in shoes not specifically designed for running; shoes that have worn down and no longer offer the cushioning, support, and stability you need; and shoes not designed for your type of foot and biomechanics. If you're selecting shoes off the rack at the discount store without knowing the type of shoe you're getting, you're asking for trouble.

How do you choose? In the next few pages we'll tell you everything you need to know before buying your shoes.

SHOO DOGGIE! AVOIDING DOG BITES

We don't have space here to address all animals that you might encounter on your runs, so we'll focus on the animal known as man's best friend: the dog.

If a dog chases you, don't try to outrun it. Instead, slow down and walk away. Don't try to stare the dog down, act threatening, or out-bark it. That just excites it.

If the dog approaches, stop and stand still. Keep the dog in sight, but don't make direct eye contact. Confrontation doesn't work. Your goal is to take away the thrill of the chase and to be uninteresting to the dog. If the same dog threatens you often, change your route and report the dog to animal control.

If the dog does attack, protect your soft tissue areas—your face, throat, and stomach. If you are bitten, report it, and find out if the dog has had rabies shots. Wash the wound well, apply antibiotic ointment, and visit the doctor.

Just remember though, not all dogs have a taste for runners.

The Right Shoes

Being familiar with these terms will help you find the right shoe for you—which translates to more miles of happy, pain-free running. When you run or walk, you land on the outside edge of your foot and roll your foot inward, which is called pronation. However, some runners roll inward too much, or not enough. Here's a guide to the terminology.

Finding the right shoes is the most important equipment decision you will make.

Normal pronation. After the outside part of your heel makes initial contact with the ground, the foot rolls inward about five percent and comes in complete contact with the ground. It can support your body weight without any problem, and the pronation optimally distributes the impact and absorbs shock. At the end of the gait cycle, you push off evenly from the front of the foot.

Overpronation. After the initial ground contact, the foot rolls inward more than the ideal five percent. The foot and ankle have problems stabilizing the body, and shock isn't absorbed as efficiently.

Then the front of the foot pushes off the ground using mainly the big toe and second toe.

Underpronation. Also called supination. After the initial ground contact, the inward movement of the foot is less than four percent. The impact is concentrated on a smaller area of the foot, the outside part, and not distributed as efficiently. In the *push-off* phase, the smaller toes on the outside of the foot do most of the work.

"The Footprint Test" on page 66 can help you determine your pronation tendencies. Here's another way to tell: Take any shoes you wear regularly, and place them on a table with the heels facing toward you. If the heels are fairly straight and tall, you pronate normally. If the heels tilt inward (toward the arches), you are probably an overpronator.

The good news is that shoes can help you control pronation problems. Here's the lowdown on types of shoes.

Cushioned shoes. These have maximum midsole cushioning and minimum arch-to-side support. They're suitable for the runner who pronates normally; these runners often have moderate to high arches. They are also suitable for underpronators.

Motion control shoes. Motion control shoes give maximum rearfoot control and extra support on the medial arch side of the foot. They're suitable for overpronators, and big or heavy runners who need plenty of support and durability. These runners often have low arches (flat feet).

Stability shoes. These supply arch-to-side support and good midsole cushioning. They are suited for runners who are mild to moderate overpronators, or need added support and durability.

HEAD FOR THE STORE

Now you have an idea what foot type you have, and are acquainted with shoe terminology. Time to get out and go shopping.

Go to a running store. Don't go to a sporting goods or department store. The staff at a running store may be trained in running and are generally much more knowledgeable about the shoes they have and what will be most suitable for you. They can study your gait and recommend appropriate running shoes.

Be prepared. Tell the salesperson how many miles you run, if you have any injuries or aches and pains, and your goals. Bring your current running shoes, the socks you usually run in, and any orthotics (shoe inserts that are molded specifically for your foot) or lifts you might use.

Get shoes that fit. Look for a shoe that gives you a little breathing space—up to 0.5 in (1.25 cm) from the longest toe to the end of the shoe. The shoe should feel snug but not tight, and the heel should not slip as you walk or run. If you have wide or narrow feet, ask for shoes that come in different widths. When you try the shoes on, the ball of your foot should line up exactly with the widest part of the shoe. Stand on one foot at a time, so you can better judge the fit. Check to see if you feel balanced in the shoes, and that the heel does not slide when you run.

Choose from a wide selection. Once you know what type of shoe you're looking for, try on several pairs and sample different brands.

Take a test run. It's critical to run in the shoes you're considering buying. Shoes that feel good while you're standing in a store might not feel good when you run in them. Ask the salesperson for permission to run briefly in the shoes. Now we understand that the store may be reticent to let you just take off down the street. But you should be able to find a spot

that suits you and doesn't worry the sales clerk. When you test them out, if you feel something about them is not quite right, that minor discrepancy may become a major nuisance later on.

Once you've found the perfect running shoes, you have dealt with the most important equipment choice you can make. As you continue to run in them, your shoes will only become more and more comfortable.

After buying your shoes, break them in on a variety of surfaces.

WATCH YOUR FORM

Running form is somewhat like snowflakes: No two are exactly alike. However, good form follows some basics. Keep these points in mind when you are running.

Head tilt. How you hold your head is key to overall posture, which determines how efficiently you run. Look ahead naturally, not down at your feet, and scan the horizon. This will straighten your neck and back.

Shoulders. Shoulders play an important role in keeping your upper body relaxed while you run. Keep your shoulders low and loose, not high and tight.

Arms. Your hands control the tension in your upper body, while your arm swing works in conjunction with your leg stride to move you forward. Keep your hands in an unclenched fist. Your arms should swing forward and back, not across your body. Your elbows should be bent at about a 90-degree angle.

Torso. Your head and shoulders affect the position of your torso. With your head up and your shoulders low and loose, your torso and back naturally straighten to let you run in an upright position that promotes optimal lung capacity and stride length.

Hips. Your hips are your center of gravity, and are key to good running posture. The proper position of your torso while running helps keep your hips in the ideal position. With your torso and back comfortably upright and straight, your hips naturally fall into proper alignment, pointing you straight ahead.

Legs and stride. Efficient endurance running requires just a slight knee lift, a quick leg turnover, and a short stride. Together, these will facilitate smooth forward movement. With the proper stride length, your feet should land directly underneath your body.

Ankles and feet. With each step, your foot should hit the ground lightly, landing between your heel and midfoot, and then quickly roll forward. Keeping your ankle flexed as your foot rolls forward creates more force for push-off. As you roll onto your toes, try to spring off the ground.

PART II:
RUNNER'S WORKOUTS

Get Flexible

The next step toward preventing running injuries and transforming yourself into a stronger, faster runner is flexibility and strength workouts. Flexibility training lets your joints and muscles move as they are supposed to when you run; strength training corrects muscle imbalances and can make you into a more explosive and powerful runner. Both will help prevent overuse injuries.

Many runners, when they're finished with their run, walk for a minute, take a shower, and get on with their day's activities. You may get away with this—for a while. But sooner or later you'll suffer from a pulled muscle or nagging pains and increasingly slower runs.

Flexibility and strength are your allies in keeping you injury free. When your muscles are strong and supple, your running technique tends to improve, and your risk of injury decreases, especially for muscle strains.

FLEXIBILITY TRAINING

What can flexibility training do for you? It can decrease your injury risk, and make you a better runner. Without flexibility, your body is a target waiting for injury to happen. Muscles cannot go through their normal ranges of motion when they are too tight, and this can lead to major injury.

The stretches depicted here target the major muscles and tendons used in running. It is advisable to do them in the order listed. During each exercise, breathe evenly through your nose. Hold each stretch for at least 15 seconds (unless otherwise noted) and repeat all stretches at least twice if possible.

It's best to do the entire set of stretching exercises at least two to three times a week, and daily is even better. If you've been troubled by a specific area, pay particular attention to that stretch.

A few points to remember:

The best time to stretch is after a run, when your muscles are warmed up and elongated.

Keep your stretching movements gradual, never jerky or hard. Stretching or pulling hard on a muscle causes shortening and tightening—the opposite of what you want.

UPPER CALF/LOWER CALF

1 Place your hands on a wall and move your right leg back two feet (0.6 m), leaning forward on your left leg, with the knee bent.

2 Straighten your right leg, keeping the right heel firmly on the floor while bringing your hip forward. Hold for at least 15 seconds. Repeat for your left leg.

TRAINER'S TIP
Calf stretches such as this one also help keep your Achilles tendons (which run from calf to heel) loose.

RUNNER'S LUNGE

1 Place your feet shoulder-width apart, with knees bent. Place your hands on the floor close to your feet.

TRAINER'S TIP
If having both legs back is awkward, this stretch can be done by alternating legs.

2 Keeping your hands on the floor, slowly bring your right foot back.

3 Fully extend your right leg behind you. Press back through your right heel to stretch the back of your knee.

4 Push up from your fingertips and bring your left leg back and heel down. Hold for at least 15 seconds.

QUADRICEPS

1 Place your right hand on the wall for support. Grasp your left foot with your left hand, bringing the foot behind you.

2 Pull your heel toward your buttocks. Hold for at least 15 seconds. Switch legs and repeat.

KNEE/ITB

1 Place your hands on your hips and cross your right foot over the left.

2 Bend forward at your hips and come down as far as you can. Hold for at least 15 seconds. Switch legs and repeat.

HAMSTRINGS

1 Lie on your back, lock your hands around your right thigh and pull your knee toward your chest.

2 Slowly extend your right foot to the ceiling until your leg is straight. Point your heel toward the ceiling. Hold for at least 15 seconds. Switch legs and repeat.

ILIOTIBIAL BAND

❶ Lie on your back, keeping your head relaxed. Bend your knees, placing your feet on the floor near your buttocks. Place the outer edge of your left foot on your right thigh near the knee.

❷ Wrap your hands around your right thigh or shin and draw it toward your chest. Hold for at least 15 seconds. Switch legs and repeat.

LEGS UP THE WALL

1 Lie down on the floor facing a wall with your hands at your sides. Extend your legs up the wall.

2 Get your buttocks as close to the wall as possible and press your lower back firmly into the floor so it is fully supported. Hold the stretch for up to five minutes.

TRAINER'S TIP
Don't hold your breath during a stretch. Try to relax and breathe evenly.

Weight-free Workout

Why do strength training if all you want to do is run? Because it will help you run faster and more efficiently—and will help you avoid injuries. Strength training strengthens your muscles and joints, so they're less likely to succumb to the stresses of running. Strength training can also correct muscle imbalances that may contribute to injuries. If your back muscles, for instance, are weak, you may slump forward when you run. If your quadriceps are stronger than your hamstrings, you may suffer hamstring injuries or knee problems.

Here we've presented two distinct groups of exercises. You can do the first group (Weight-free Workout) at home or in a gym, preferably before running, two to three times a week (see specific exercise for number of repetitions). The second group (Strength Training) requires weights and a stability ball, and should be done two to three times a week.

For this first group, you'll need a piece of resistive tubing, available from pharmacies with home-therapy sections or from companies that sell sports-medicine products. Some of the exercises also include a step or bench which can be found in any gym or purchased at your local sporting goods shop.

This first workout is great because of the limited equipment you'll need to execute all of the

moves, which are low impact. Each one of these exercises builds muscle and also strengthens joints and connective tissues. This is important in preventing injury, because the repetitive nature of running can put stress on those joints and tissues.

For best results, do these exercises before you run. Within a few weeks you'll notice improved coordination during running and more explosive push-offs when your feet strike the ground. As your muscles become more powerful, risk of injury will decrease, and your running speed will improve significantly.

A final word on strength training. If you feel these routines are in any way inhibiting your running, cut back on the frequency with which you perform them.

HIP HIKER

TARGET: Buttocks and hips

1 Stand on a step or low bench with your weight on your left leg and your right leg over the edge of the step. Keep your legs straight throughout the exercise.

2 Lower your right heel toward the floor by tilting your right hip down. Keep your left leg straight. Raise your right hip as high as it will go. Repeat 12 times. Switch legs.

RESISTED LEG SWING

TARGET: Hamstrings and lower leg

1. Anchor one end of a piece of resistive tubing at hip height to an immovable object. Place the other end of the tubing around your right ankle and stretch the tubing about 4 feet (1.2 m) from the attachment point, facing the point.

2. Shift your body weight to your left leg and stand on your left foot only. Raise your right thigh parallel to the floor and move your right leg through a normal running motion 10 times.

3. Don't touch your right foot to the floor at any point during the cycle. Switch legs and repeat.

TRAINER'S TIP

Having trouble keeping your balance? Lightly steady yourself on a stationary object with one hand. Don't lean.

TOE PRESSES

TARGET: Calf and Achilles tendon

① Stand on a step with your weight on the ball of your left foot and your left heel hanging down below the edge of the step. Bend your right leg. Keep your balance by holding onto a rail or placing your hand on a wall.

② Rise up as high as you can on the toes of your left foot, keeping your left leg straight. Lower your left heel below the level of the step. Repeat 15 times and switch to the right leg.

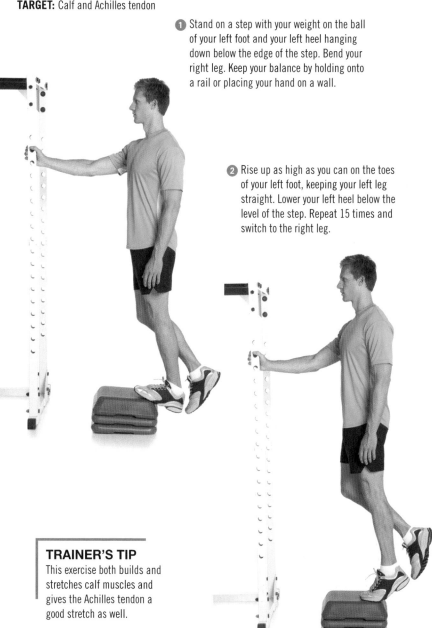

TRAINER'S TIP
This exercise both builds and stretches calf muscles and gives the Achilles tendon a good stretch as well.

BENCH STEP-UPS
TARGET: Buttocks and hamstrings

1 Begin from a standing position on top of a bench of about knee height. Put all your body weight on your left foot. Maintain an upright posture with your hands at your sides. Hang your right foot slightly behind your body.

TRAINER'S TIP
When executing bench step-ups, it is important to keep your weight on whichever foot is on the bench.

2 Lower your body until the toes of the right foot touch the ground. Return to the starting position by pushing down with your left heel and straightening your left leg. Repeat 10 times and switch legs.

ONE-LEG SQUATS
TARGET: Quadriceps

1 Stand with your feet hip-width apart, with your left foot forward and your right foot back. Place the toes of your right foot on a block or step that is 6 to 8 inches (15–20 cm) high.

2 Bend your left leg and lower your body until your left knee is at a 90-degree angle. Repeat the exercise 10 times and then do the same for your right leg.

TRAINER'S TIP
Throughout this exercise, make sure to keep your trunk upright and your hands at your sides.

ONE-LEG HOPS

TARGET: Hips, thighs, lower legs

1 Start with the toes of your right foot supported on a 6- to 8-inch (15–20-cm) block or step. Hop rapidly on your left foot, raising your left knee 4 to 6 inches (10–15 cm) each time. Touch down in the midfoot region and then spring upward as rapidly as possible.

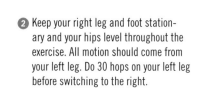

2 Keep your right leg and foot stationary and your hips level throughout the exercise. All motion should come from your left leg. Do 30 hops on your left leg before switching to the right.

ABDOMINAL STABILIZERS

TARGET: Abdominals and obliques

1 Sit on a bench or chair and extend your legs in front of you, slightly bending your knees. Move your upper torso so it is at about a 45-degree angle from your hips.

TRAINER'S TIP
Keep your upper torso and legs stiff throughout the exercise. Only your arms should move.

2 Raise your left arm over your head, holding it straight, while lowering your right arm. Alternate until you have raised each arm 30 times.

Strength Training

Typical weight workouts—bench presses, biceps curls, and leg extensions—don't help you as a runner. Standard weight-lifting routines may increase your risk of injury, because the typical workout often creates strength imbalances in muscle groups. These routines, however, target key muscle groups, and keep them balanced.

The following strengthening routines require weights and a stability ball, which could mean a trip to the gym (unless you have a well-stocked home workout room). These are designed to be done in two separate sessions, requiring about 30 minutes each, and each should be done once a week.

Each session has five exercises. Do each session once a week, with at least one day in between. Use the heaviest weight that lets you finish every set. If you finish the last set feeling like you could have done five more repetitions, you need to use a heavier weight.

The first workout here covers the exercises on pages 41 through 45. Let's call it Workout A. Perform the first three exercises (Overhead Lunge, Mixed Grip Chin-up, and Scorpion) as a circuit, doing one set each before moving to the next. Try and do at least two circuits. Alternate between the final two

exercises (Stability-Ball Jackknife and Back Extension with Lower Trap Raise) until you've done two or three sets.

The second workout covers the exercises on pages 46 through 50. We'll call this one Workout B. Much the same as Workout A, the first three exercises here (Stability-Ball Leg-Hip Extension with Leg Curl, Rotational Shoulder Press, and Stability Ball Knee Drive) should be treated like a circuit and done at least twice. The last two exercises (Alternating Dumbbell Row and Lower Body Russian Twist) you should again alternate until you've done two or three sets.

Most of the exercises within these workouts contain recommendations for how many repetitions you should do. If you find yourself struggling to make the maximum number of reps, start with fewer and work your way up as you get stronger. As with any type of training, patience is key.

OVERHEAD LUNGE

TARGET: Quadriceps, hamstrings, gluteus, shoulders, and core

❶ Hold a pair of dumbbells straight above your head, locking your elbows and keeping your arms straight.

❷ Step forward with your left leg and lower your body until your knee is bent 90 degrees. Return to the starting position, and repeat with your right leg. Do six to eight repetitions per leg.

MIXED GRIP CHIN-UP

TARGET: Back, biceps, and core

1 Grab the chin-up bar overhand with your right hand, and underhand with your left. Hang with your arms completely straight.

2 Pull yourself as high as you can without allowing your body to rotate. Do six to eight times. Alternate grips each set.

TRAINER'S TIP

To make it easier, place a bench underneath the bar. Jump up to the top position, then lower yourself slowly.

SCORPION
TARGET: Shoulders and core

1 Get into a pushup position, but with your feet on a bench.

2 Raise your left knee toward your right shoulder as you rotate your hips up and to the right as far as you can.

3 Reverse direction by rotating your hips up and to the left. Do as many times as you can in 30 seconds, then switch legs.

STABILITY-BALL JACKKNIFE

TARGET: Shoulders and core

1 Get into pushup position with your shins on a stability ball, instead of placing your feet on the floor.

2 Pull the stability ball toward your chest by raising your hips and rounding your back as you roll the ball forward with your feet. Repeat 10 to 12 times.

BACK EXTENSION WITH LOWER TRAP RAISE

TARGET: Lower and middle back, gluteus, and shoulders

1 Holding two dumbbells, position yourself in the back-extension station. Lower your upper body until it's almost parallel to the floor. Hang your arms down from your shoulders, your palms facing each other.

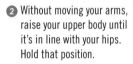

2 Without moving your arms, raise your upper body until it's in line with your hips. Hold that position.

3 Raise your arms until they're in line with your torso and form a "Y." Lower your arms slowly and repeat the entire move. Do 10 to 12 repetitions.

STABILITY-BALL LEG-HIP EXTENSION WITH LEG CURL

TARGET: Hamstrings, gluteus, and core

1 Lie on your back on the floor and place your calves on a stability ball. Extend your arms to your sides.

2 Push your hips up so that your body forms a straight line from your shoulders to your knees.

3 Roll the ball as close as you can to your hips by pulling your heels toward you. Do six to eight times.

ROTATIONAL SHOULDER PRESS

TARGET: Shoulders, triceps, and core

1 Stand holding a pair of dumbbells just outside your shoulders, with your elbows bent and your palms facing out. Raise your arms overhead as you rotate to your left.

2 Lower the dumbbells as you rotate back to the center, and then rotate to the right as you press the weights upward again. Repeat six to eight times.

TRAINER'S TIP
Contract your abdominal muscles to stabilize your core. Keep your back flat and straight.

STABILITY-BALL KNEE DRIVE
TARGET: Shoulders and core

1 Put your hands on a stability ball and get into a pushup position. Form a straight line from your shoulders to your ankles. Keep your arms straight.

2 Quickly raise your left knee as close as you can to your chest. Lower it and repeat with your right leg. Do this as many times as you can in 30 seconds.

ALTERNATING DUMBBELL ROW

TARGET: Middle back, biceps, and core

1 Hold a pair of dumbbells at arm's length in front of you, with your palms facing your thighs. Keep your back naturally arched and bend at the hips, lowering your torso until it's nearly parallel to the floor.

2 Pull the dumbbell in your right hand by bending your elbow and raising your upper arm toward the middle of your back. Lower and repeat with your left arm. Do 10 to 12 times.

TRAINER'S TIP

This exercise can also be done piston-style where you raise one arm as you are lowering the other.

LOWER BODY RUSSIAN TWIST

TARGET: Core

1 Lie on your back with your upper legs perpendicular to the floor and your knees bent 90 degrees. Place your arms flat at your sides.

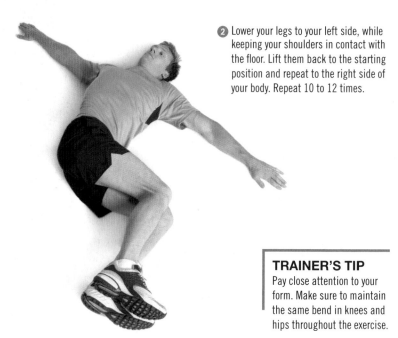

2 Lower your legs to your left side, while keeping your shoulders in contact with the floor. Lift them back to the starting position and repeat to the right side of your body. Repeat 10 to 12 times.

TRAINER'S TIP

Pay close attention to your form. Make sure to maintain the same bend in knees and hips throughout the exercise.

PART III
INJURIES

Heat Injuries

Heat injury comes in two main forms: heat exhaustion and heatstroke. Heat exhaustion is overheating from loss of water and sometimes from lack of salt. Heatstroke, which can be fatal if not treated, occurs when your body can no longer regulate its temperature.

RECOGNIZING

Heat exhaustion symptoms may include extreme thirst, dizziness, paleness, nausea, vomiting, weakness, lack of coordination, headache, high body temperature, cool, clammy skin, racing heart, and disorientation.

Heatstroke symptoms are similar, but may include little to no sweating, difficulty walking, hot and dry skin, and severe headache.

TREATING

For heat exhaustion, stop running and get out of the sun and, preferably, into an air-conditioned building. Drink water or a sports drink. Remove extra clothing. If you suspect heatstroke, also pack ice around the neck, armpits, and groin. Splash cold water on the skin and fan the runner. Elevate the legs and give fluids. As soon as possible, head to the hospital.

On hot days try to avoid running in those hours when the sun is at its peak.

RECOVERING

Most runners recover from heat exhaustion within 12 to 48 hours. Wait at least one day, drinking plenty of fluids, before running again.

Recovery from heatstroke takes longer and depends on the damage done. If you have suffered heatstroke, don't run until your doctor clears you to do so.

PREVENTING

• Keep hydrated! Drink plenty of fluids before, during, and after runs in hot or humid weather.

• Run in early morning when it's coolest. Late evening is the next best choice. Avoid mid-morning to early-evening runs if at all possible, and definitely don't run at the hottest times of the day.

• Wear cool, light-colored clothing that allows perspiration out and breeze in. Wear a cool, light cap. And don't forget the sunscreen!

• Run shorter distances.

• Replenish what you lose. Use a sports drink to replenish lost minerals; many fruits and vegetables—bananas, watermelon, cantaloupe, carrots, and tomatoes—offer a great way to replace both fluids and minerals.

• If you begin feeling any symptoms of heat illness, stop running. Get out of the sun. Hydrate.

TOO MUCH WATER?

As strange as it sounds, it's possible to overdose on water. *Hyponatremia* (water intoxication) occurs when the body's water and sodium levels get out of balance, generally due to too much water consumption. This usually happens only during long, hot runs, when a runner loses sodium through sweating and drinks a lot of plain water.

Early symptoms are similar to those of dehydration: confusion, disorientation, muscle weakness, and vomiting. Hyponatremia can trigger seizures, coma, and lead to death.

To avoid this problem, include salt in your normal diet, particularly a few days before a long event. Also, drink sports drinks rather than plain water on runs that last longer than an hour. And don't drink more than 16 to 24 ounces of fluid within an hour of racing or going on a long run.

Cold Injuries

When running in cold weather, be aware of the risks of *hypothermia*, which occurs when your body temperature drops below 96°F (36°C), and *frostbite*, damage that occurs when your extremities begin to freeze. In extreme conditions, hypothermia can be fatal, and frostbite can do severe and lasting damage to your body.

RECOGNIZING

Hypothermia symptoms include drowsiness, weakness and loss of coordination, pale and cold skin, confusion, uncontrollable shivering (although, at extremely low body temperatures, shivering may stop), and slowed breathing or heart rate.

Frostbite symptoms include hard, pale, cold skin; lack of sensitivity to the touch; aching pain in the affected area, and as the skin thaws, it will become red and quite painful.

TREATING

If you have symptoms of either hypothermia or frostbite, move into a warm place as soon as possible. Remove any wet clothing. Seek medical attention.

If immediate medical help is not available, and there is no risk that the area might get refrozen before you get help, immerse the affected areas in warm water, or apply warm cloths to those same spots. Do this for 20 to 30 minutes. You may experience severe burning pain, swelling, and color changes as your skin is warmed. Do *not* rub or massage the affected area. Do *not* walk on frostbitten feet or toes. Do *not* apply direct dry heat (such as with a hair dryer) to the affected skin. This can cause more damage.

RECOVERING

If you have suffered either hypothermia or frostbite, get your doctor's approval before resuming running. The recovery period depends on the individual and the severity of the injury.

In cases of hypothermia, if your body temperature did not drop below 90°F (32°C) chances of a full recovery are good. With frostbite recovery, patience is the key. Make sure you stay away from things that will interfere with blood circulation, such as drinking alcohol or smoking.

Don't let a little snow get between you and your running regimen.

PREVENTING

• Layer your clothing and wear a wicking layer next to your skin.

• Wear mittens instead of gloves. Consider disposable heat packets inside your mittens.

• Wear a hat that covers your ears or a facemask.

• Wear running socks made partially of wool.

• Use a scarf or neck warmer to keep the wind from exposed areas on your neck.

• Choose synthetic fibers that wick moisture away from your skin—avoid cotton.

• Use petroleum jelly to help protect exposed skin on your face.

• If the weather is extremely cold and windy, don't run outside.

• Carry a sports drink (dehydration makes you more prone to hypothermia).

• If you get caught in a severe storm, find shelter and ride it out. The less exposure, the better.

Muscle Pulls

Muscle tears—sometimes called "pulls" because of a pulling sensation in the torn muscle—can happen from a one-time incident or from chronic overuse. The classic acute tear occurs during sprinting, and cold weather. Inadequate warming up, limited flexibility, or imbalance between the quadriceps and the hamstrings can all contribute.

RECOGNIZING

Acute muscle tears are accompanied by searing pain. The muscle spasms, is tender to the touch, and can't function normally. Swelling occurs, though it might not be discernable.

Chronic muscle tears will have a gradual onset of pain. The pain is usually deep and generally feels worse during more intense workouts, and may not be present at rest. If someone feels a knot when pressing firmly with two

WHEN YOUR STYLE GETS CRAMPED

Muscle cramps can be both humbling and painful. A cramp is an involuntary contraction that stays contracted. Generally, your calves, hamstrings, and quadriceps are most susceptible.

No one knows for sure what causes them, but possibilities include heat, dehydration, low electrolytes, muscle fatigue, inadequate training, and lack of stretching. Here's how to help avoid them:

• Stretch regularly, paying particular attention to your calves, hamstrings, and quadriceps.

• Have a sports drink an hour or two before you run, which will boost your electrolyte level. Drink every 15 to 20 minutes during your run.

• Add plyometrics—leaping, hopping, and skipping drills—to your training. These can improve muscle-nerve coordination and strength and help loosen tight muscles.

If you do get a cramp, stop and gently stretch the cramping muscle. Keep stretching, applying pressure to the muscle by pushing in with your fingers until the cramp stops.

fingers into the affected muscle, and your pain increases, you have a chronic muscle tear.

TREATING

Rest and relieve inflammation by icing four or five times a day for 20 minutes at a time, and by taking an anti-inflammatory such as ibuprofen or aspirin. There are also a number of over-the-counter muscle ache ointments that you can find at your local pharmacy.

RECOVERING

When your pain subsides, begin a gentle stretching regimen. Stretch to the point where you feel some tension, but not beyond. This stretching may also decrease the chances of scar tissue forming.

If the tear doesn't heal soon, see a sports doctor. More aggressive treatments by physical therapists and athletic trainers may be needed.

How quickly you recover depends on your age, the severity of the pull, how you respond to it, and whether the pull is an acute or chronic. Chronic tears are harder to overcome, and if you are chronically injuring a certain muscle, see a sports doctor to discuss ways to reduce the chances of reinjuring it.

PREVENTING

• Warm up and stretch adequately. This is especially crucial for speed workouts and hard runs.
• Correct any muscular imbalances, especially between your quadriceps and hamstrings (see page 32). You can have your muscular balance assessed by a physical therapist.
• Have a sports physical therapist assess your running form for problems that may contribute to hamstring pulls.

Stretching before and after runs is the key to avoiding muscle pulls and tears.

Back Pain

Back pain is common—about 70 percent of adults suffer moderate or severe back pain at some point (and often multiple points) in their lives. The pain can result from disc degeneration between the vertebrae in the lower back or from damage to back muscles, ligaments, or joints. Running stresses the lower back, and excessive pronation, imbalance between the abdominal and back muscles, and inflexible hamstrings increases the potential for back injury.

Keeping back muscles limber can go a long way in helping avoid serious injuries.

Chronic muscle tears in the glutei or piriformis muscles can be felt in the lower back. Pain that begins in your lower back and shoots down one of your legs is *sciatica*, irritation caused by stress on that nerve, which runs from your lower back down your legs.

RECOGNIZING

A single-incident injury is simple enough to recognize: Your back muscles cramp and you feel excruciating pain. In severe cases, you're unable to walk or straighten up. With back problems that are less severe and more chronic, you may feel a stiffness or mild soreness. But any discomfort in your back can be debilitating.

With sciatica, you feel pain shooting down your leg, which may feel like burning or an electrical sensation.

TREATING

How you treat your back pain depends on the nature of the injury. If you can't move without severe pain or have chronic problems, see a doctor. For mild pain, ice four or five times a day, 20 minutes at a time. (Simply place the ice bag on your bed or the floor, and lie on it.) Some people find relief with a cold/hot regimen, alternating 20 minutes of cold with 20 minutes of heat. Try sleeping with a pillow between your legs when lying on your side, and two pillows under your legs when sleeping on your back.

Sciatica, irritation in the sciatic nerve, can run from your buttocks all the way down to your foot. For this type of pain don't ice; take an anti-inflammatory such as ibuprofen or aspirin and do the stretching program on pages 24 to 31. If the pain persists for more than 10 days or so, see a sports-oriented doctor (sciatica may be caused by a leg-length discrepancy that can sometimes be alleviated and corrected with physical therapy or orthotics).

RECOVERING

If running doesn't make your back pain worse, go ahead and run. Choose soft surfaces and avoid hills and irregular surfaces. If running does start to make the pain worse or is too painful, try swimming, cycling, walking, or running in a pool.

The recovery period depends on the cause. A degenerative disc can be serious, and you will need to consult a doctor for this type of injury. Surgery is the last line of defense against this type of condition, and can usually be avoided.

If your pain is from an acute injury, most often you can recover within two weeks or less. You can shorten the time by applying the ice as recommended the first three days and taking an anti-inflammatory such as ibuprofen or aspirin.

PREVENTING

• Strengthen your core muscles: your abdominals, trunk, and back muscles (see pages 40–50).
• Stretch your back muscles and hamstrings (see pages 29–31); many back injuries occur because the muscles are tight and inflexible.

• Strengthen your abdominal muscles (see page 39); with weak abdominals, your back muscles have to carry more of the workload.

• Have a sports physical therapist or podiatrist check your biomchanics.

Your running form might be putting undue stress on your back (you may run with a pronounced forward lean, for example).

• Schedule an evaluation by a podiatrist to see if you need orthotics.

IF THIS IS MONDAY, I MUST BE SORE

You ran a race on Saturday morning and wonder how sore you will be when Sunday arrives. After all, you've never run so hard over this much distance.

But you're not sore at all. In fact, your legs feel great.

Monday you wake up wondering if someone dropped a load of weights on your legs while you were sleeping.

You're a victim of delayed onset muscle soreness. This tends to come on after hard running—a track workout, a race, running hard on hills, especially downhill. It's caused by muscle protein breakdown, resulting in cell inflammation, which activates pain sensors around the muscle fibers. It typically comes on 24 to 72 hours after the event, but most often it's worse during hours 48 to 72.

What can you do to prevent it?

• Warm up properly, and gradually increase the intensity and duration of your workouts.

• At the end of a hard run, walk rather than stop completely. If possible, cool your legs off with cold water over the entire leg.

• Take an anti-inflammatory such as ibuprofen or aspirin.

• Stretch often and, if possible, get a massage.

• After running a marathon, take three days off from running and cycle instead.

• Add some downhill running to your training every two to three weeks, especially when you're preparing for a downhill race.

In the meantime, try some non-pounding aerobic exercise, such as walking or cycling to get your blood moving.

ITB–Iliotibial Band Syndrome

The iliotibial band (ITB) is a thick strip of connective tissue that runs down the outside of your thigh from the hip to the shin immediately below the knee joint. Where the band is near the knee, it narrows, and rubbing can occur between the ITB and the bone, causing inflammation.

Downhill running can occasionally be the cause of iliotibial band irritation.

ITB syndrome can result from any activity that causes the leg to turn inward, such as wearing old worn-down shoes, running downhill or on a banked surface, and doing too many miles. Overpronation, underpronation, and inflexibility can also stress the ITB. It works to stabilize your knee, and the pulling results in pain and inflammation.

RECOGNIZING

You'll feel a dull ache on the outside of your knee, usually a mile or so into a run, which disappears soon after you stop. You may feel severe pain, but not typically at rest or during other physical activity. The pain spikes during downhill running, and can also be felt walking downstairs. Another symptom is extreme tenderness in the outside part of the knee, especially when the knee is flexed to about 30 degrees.

TREATING

Reduce inflammation with ice and an anti-inflammatory such as ibuprofen or aspirin. Replace your running shoes and use orthotics if needed to control pronation. Work on flexibility of the ITB, calf, and hamstring (see pages 25–31. Ultrasound technology has often helped runners recover from this syndrome.

RECOVERING

Trying to run through this injury will only prolong it. Do not run through pain. This injury is one of the most difficult to treat, and its recovery can sometimes be exasperatingly slow.

Absolutely cut back on speed work, and don't run downhill. Add cross training such as cycling, swimming, or running in a pool, and work on flexibility exercises. This injury can take anywhere from a few weeks to several months to clear up. The earlier you treat it, the more likely you will recover quickly and be back on the road.

PREVENTING

• Stretch your iliotibial band (see page 28).
• Do your calf flexibility exercises (see page 35).
• Do your hamstring flexibility exercises (see page 34).
• Be sure to choose the right shoes for you (see pages 19–21).
• Replace shoes when worn out.
• Decrease mileage or take a few days off if you feel pain on the outside of your knee.
• Walk for a few minutes before you start your runs.
• Replace your shoes if they are worn along the outside of the sole.
• Be sure to run on flat surfaces and avoid concrete.
• When running on a track, change directions repeatedly.
• Schedule an evaluation by a podiatrist to see if you need orthotics.
• Avoid running on banked surfaces, such as crowned roads, the beach, or a track. If you do run on a track, split your time running clockwise and counterclockwise.
• Try to avoid any sudden increases in mileage.

Runner's Knee

This affliction, also called chondromalacia patella and patellofemoral pain syndrome, is the most common over-use running injury. It occurs when a kneecap (patella) isn't tracking as it should. Because the kneecap deviates to one side, the cartilage that lines the underside of the kneecap softens and eventually develops tears and cracks.

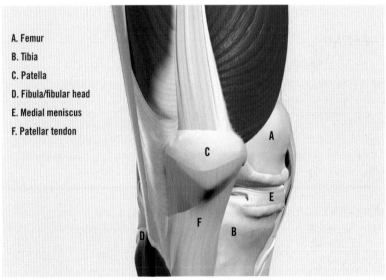

A. Femur

B. Tibia

C. Patella

D. Fibula/fibular head

E. Medial meniscus

F. Patellar tendon

This diagram shows the normal position of the patella (C, above) which is where runner's knee occurs.

The cause could be a biomechanical problem: The patella may be larger on the outside than it is on the inside or it may sit too high in the groove. Other possible causes: worn cartilage in the knee joint, which reduces shock absorption; high-arched feet, which provide less cushioning; and flat feet or knees that turn in or out excessively, which can pull the patella sideways. Also, tight hamstring and calf muscles put pressure on the knee, and weak quadriceps muscles can cause the patella to track out of alignment. It affects twice as many women as men, because women's wider hips results in a greater angling of the thigh-bone to the knee, which stresses the kneecap. This is a common injury for many runners.

RECOGNIZING

Symptoms include tenderness behind or around the kneecap, usually toward its center. You may feel pain toward the back of the knee, a sense of cracking or that the knee is giving out. Steps, hills, and uneven terrain can aggravate it.

A good way to test for runner's knee is to lie down with your legs relaxed. Have someone raise the top of your kneecap so that the bottom portion of the cap lifts off the knee joint. With their other hand, this person should apply firm pressure with two fingers to the exposed area under the kneecap. If this pressure produces pain, you likely have runner's knee.

TREATING

At the first sign of pain, reduce your mileage. The sooner you decrease the stress on your knee, the sooner it can begin to heal. (If the pain is severe, do not run.) Avoid any knee-bending activities, stairs, and slopes until the pain is gone.

Reduce inflammation with an anti-inflammatory such as ibuprofen or aspirin, taken about 30 minutes before you run. Apply ice two or three times for 20 minutes

Icing your injury after you run will help reduce inflammation.

at a time after you run. Keep your leg elevated when possible, or stretched out, and avoid weight-bearing activities if possible.

Have a gait analysis done. Be fitted for shoes that correct any mechanical problems with your gait (if you pronate excessively, for instance). Consider orthotics.

Do stretching and strengthening exercises aimed at increasing the flexibility of your hamstrings and calves and at strengthening your quadriceps.

RECOVERING

Runner's knee is one of those injuries that is tempting to run through. The discomfort, at least in the beginning, is mild, though it generally does get worse the longer you run without treating the injury. Do your best to ignore your tendencies to tough it out and deal with the pain.

The immediate objective is to reduce inflammation, which won't happen with continued running. For mild to moderate cases, a week or two off, coupled with other treatments, may be adequate. Other cases may require four to six weeks of active rest. If you are still experiencing pain, you're not healed and should probably contact your physician.

You can maintain your fitness level, however, by water running, swimming, cycling in low gear, or spinning. Do any activity that doesn't put stress on your knee.

When you return to running, begin slowly and use a smaller stride on hills. This can be difficult, because you're raring to go and your cardiovascular system can handle more than the light mileage that you need to return to. But you must start slowly. Supplement your lighter mileage with cross training. You can still get in the total amount of work you want to; you just won't put all that workload on your just-healed knee. Err on the side of caution.

PREVENTING

- Choose the right shoes for you.
- Replace shoes when worn out.
- Schedule an evaluation by a podiatrist to see if you need orthotics.
- Run on softer surfaces.
- Increase your mileage no more than 10 percent per week.
- Add hill work gradually.
- Avoid downhill running.
- Strengthen your quadriceps (see pages 37 and 41).
- Stretch your hamstrings and calves (see pages 25–31).
- Stretch your quadriceps (see page 28).

THE FOOTPRINT TEST

Many running injuries can be traced to faulty footwear. The best way to find out what type of shoe you need is to see an expert in running biomechanics, such as a podiatrist. But if you want a quick estimate, try this: First, step with your wet bare foot on a piece of paper. Observe the shape of your foot and match it with one of these descriptions. Although other variables such as your weight and weekly mileage come into play, knowing your foot type is the first step toward selecting the right shoe.

Normal (medium) arch. If you see about half of your arch, but your footprint remains connected from heel to toe, you have healthy, normal pronation (rolling inward as the foot hits the ground). This pronation absorbs shock, and a normal pronator can wear just about any shoe. The best choice, however, may be a stability shoe that provides moderate arch support (or medial stability). Lightweight runners with normal arches may prefer cushioned shoes without any added support, or a performance-training shoe that offers some support but less heft.

Flat (low) arch. If you see almost your entire footprint, you have a flat foot, which means you probably overpronate. After your foot hits the ground, your arch collapses inward too much, causing excessive foot motion and increasing your risk of injuries. If you are a mild to moderate overpronator, you need stability shoes, which use dual-density midsoles and supportive "posts" to reduce pronation. If you are a severe overpronator, tall and heavy (more than 165 pounds/75 kg), or are bow legged, you need motion control shoes, which offer firmer support.

High arch. If you see just your heel, the ball of your foot, and a thin line on the outside of your foot, you have a high arch, the least common foot type. This means you're likely an underpronator, or supinator, which can result in too much shock traveling up your leg because your arch doesn't collapse enough to absorb the shock. Underpronators need the softer midsole of cushioned shoes to encourage pronation.

Shinsplints

Shinsplints, an inflammation of the tendons on the inside of the front of the lower leg, are one of the most common running injuries. They result from tired or inflexible calf muscles putting too much stress on the tendons, which become strained. Overpronating aggravates the condition, as does running on hard surfaces, such as concrete, and running in shoes that are too stiff. (Some people use the term "shinsplints" to refer to all shin pain of any origin, including other lower-leg injuries such as stress fractures or inflammation of the bone covering. Here, we are referring only to tendinitis of the lower leg.)

Beginning runners are the most susceptible to shinsplints, partly because their leg muscles aren't used to the stress. Runners who have started running after long lay-offs are also susceptible, because they often increase their mileage too quickly.

RECOGNIZING

You may feel an aching, throbbing, or tenderness along the inside of the shin (although it can also radiate to the outside) about halfway down or all along the shin, from your ankle to your knee. As the injury progresses, the discomfort increases and the pain can become quite severe. If you grit your teeth and continue running through this pain, you eventually will feel it even when walking.

Another symptom is pain when pressing on the inflamed area. The pain is worse at the start of a run, but can go away during a

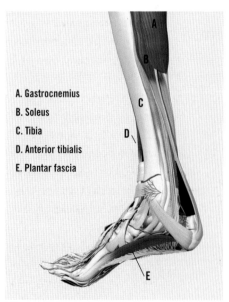

A. Gastrocnemius
B. Soleus
C. Tibia
D. Anterior tibialis
E. Plantar fascia

Inflamed anterior tibial tendons (D, above) are the primary cause of shinsplints.

Shorter, more compact strides help reduce the amount of stress on your shins.

run once the muscles are loosened up (unlike a stress fracture, which will hurt all of the time). With tendinitis, pain will resume after the run.

TREATING

Cut down on running or stop altogether. Ice the inflamed area for 15 minutes three times a day and take an anti-inflammatory such as ibuprofen or aspirin. Ice for 20 minutes immediately after you run.

If the injury doesn't respond to self-treatment and rest in two to four weeks, see a podiatrist, who may recommend orthotics to control overpronation.

Have a gait analysis done. Be fitted for shoes that correct any mechanical problems with your gait (if you pronate excessively, for instance). Consider finding out if you need orthotics.

Have someone check your running form. If you overstride, or if your feet slap the ground too hard, you overwork the muscles in the front of your calves, causing pain in your tibia.

RECOVERING

Your recovery period can be brief if you treat the splints early and effectively. You may not need to miss any training, just reduce your workload.

With more severe cases, you will have to cut back or stop running. While recovering from shin-splints, try non-impact exercises such as swimming, running in a pool, walking, and cycling in a low gear. Generally, you should be able to return to running within two to three weeks, though in severe cases you might be out four to six weeks.

PREVENTING

• Increase your mileage no more than 10 percent per week.
• Incorporate speed work gradually—it increases the loading stress on the shin muscles.
• Never increase mileage and speed work at the same time.
• Avoid overstriding, which stresses your shins.
• If needed, wear stability or motion control shoes.
• Schedule an evaluation with a podiatrist concerning orthotics.
• Replace shoes when worn out.
• Run on soft surfaces.
• Stretch your calf muscles (see pages 25–27).
• Stretch your Achilles tendons (see page 35).
• Strengthen your lower leg with band exercises (see page 34).

STITCHES

A stitch is a sharp pain, usually felt just below your ribs. It is usually brought on by a spasm in the diaphragm, caused by shallow and rapid breathing.

For a stitch on the right side, slow down for 30 seconds, exhaling forcefully when your left foot hits the ground. (Reverse if the stitch is on your left side.) If the stitch persists, breathe deeply through your belly, with your abdomen moving in and out with each breath. You can also try running with your hands on top of your head and your elbows back while you do this.

Alternatively, place your fist under your ribcage, and push upward to relive the strain on the diaphragm, and bend your torso to almost 90 degrees. Breathe evenly as you do so. Run for 10 steps.

If it still hurts, lying on the ground on your back with your legs elevated should do the trick (and amuse any passersby as well; but who cares, if it relieves the pain?).

Toenail Problems

Toenails are something you seldom think about—unless one hurts. Then it grabs all your attention. Problems you might encounter include ingrown nails, black toenails, runner's nail, and fungal toenails. We'll focus on the first two. (Runner's nail refers to thickened nails that also can become discolored, which should cause you little discomfort unless they become infected. Fungal toenails are—you guessed it—toenails infected by fungus. If you suspect you have an infection, see your doctor or a podiatrist for treatment options.)

RECOGNIZING

With ingrown nails, the nail curves and grows into the side of the toe. You will feel pain and the affected area may be red and swollen. All nails curve down at the sides, but an ingrown nail curves more severely and puts excessive pressure against the skin. Ingrown nails may be caused by clipping the nail too short or excessive pressure from the forefront of the shoe. The constant pressure results in inflammation, and the nail can break the skin and cause infection.

Black toenails, a common ailment among runners, especially long distance runners, are aptly named. Black toenails are caused by a pooling of blood under the nail. This can happen from a single, traumatic incident (such as dropping a weight on your toe), but is more likely to occur from repetitive motion of the toe rubbing against the shoe. The toe may throb from the pressure of the blood.

TREATING

For ingrown nails, try soaking the affected foot in Epsom salts and use an antifungal cream on the ingrown nail. Some minor ingrown nails correct themselves. Most ingrown toenails, however, tend to be quite painful, and should be treated by a podiatrist. Don't try to relieve the pressure of an infected nail yourself by cutting or trimming or by any other method.

In most cases you don't need to treat a black toenail. Lubricate it with antifungal cream and cover it with a bandage. The nail will probably loosen and fall off over

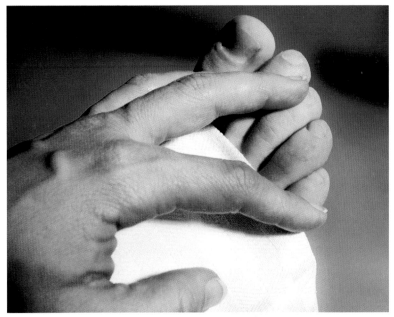
Untreated toenail problems can often lead to more serious injury or infection.

the next few months. When it gets loose, pull it off and continue to apply the antifungal cream. The toenail bed can be quite painful for a few to several days. If the black toenail is painful and you need to relieve the pressure, see a sports-oriented physician.

RECOVERING
For both ingrown nails and black toenails, recovery depends on your pain. If you've had a procedure to relieve the pressure or remove the nail, you should be able to resume running very quickly (but check with the person who performed the procedure). For most black toenail cases you experience pain for a few to several days and discomfort for a few more, and then your toe is not painful at all. (If this isn't the case with yours, or if you see redness mixed in with the black discoloration, see a doctor.)

PREVENTING
• To avoid ingrown nails, don't cut your nails too short or wear shoes that are too small.
• To avoid black toenails, wear well-fitting shoes. Buy shoes either after you've run, or in the late afternoon or evening when your feet will be more swollen so you'll get a truer fit.

Achilles Tendonitis

This heel pain occurs when your Achilles tendon becomes inflamed. This large tendon connects your major calf muscles to your heel bone. The act of running causes these calf muscles and the Achilles tendon to tighten, and when the tendon is working too hard, it can become stiff, tender, and sore. In time, it can produce a covering of inflexible scar tissue, and the tendon can tear or rupture if you keep working it. Overpronation may increase the risk of Achilles tendon injuries, because the tendon twists as the foot rolls inward.

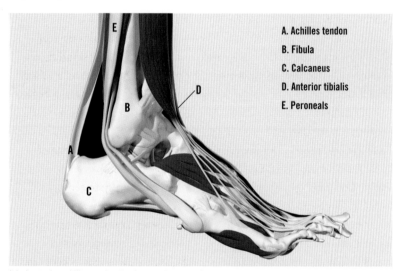

A. Achilles tendon

B. Fibula

C. Calcaneus

D. Anterior tibialis

E. Peroneals

Injuries to the achilles tendon (A, above), which runs from the calf down to the heel, can be slow to heal.

RECOGNIZING

You'll notice this injury immediately when you step out of bed in the morning: the tendon is quite stiff and is tender to the touch. You'll feel dull or sharp pain along the tendon, usually close to your heel. Your ankle will likely be less flexible, and the painful area may be red or feel warm. You may hear a crackling sound when your ankle moves. In the early stages, this stiffness wears off after five or 10 minutes and the discomfort is minimal. As the injury progresses, you'll notice soreness in the tendon after (but not during) your runs. This is particularly true after longer runs or track workouts. You'll also notice discomfort when walking uphill or upstairs.

TREATING

You must treat Achilles problems quickly, before excessive tearing or scarring occurs. Because the Achilles tendon has relatively little blood flow, it can be difficult to heal. Ignoring it in the early stages makes it worse, and may lead to scarring and tearing or could rupture. Stop running. Continuing to run with an inflamed Achilles tendon can cause it to tear.

Control the inflammation with an anti-inflammatory such as ibuprofen or aspirin. Ice the area for 15 to 20 minutes several times a day. Self-massage may also help: rub semicircles in all directions away from the knotted tissue, three times a day.

If you're not better in two weeks, consult a physical therapist or orthopedic surgeon. If your tendon has ruptured or has built up much scar tissue, you may need a cast or surgery. (Note: If you stop running and immediately treat your inflamed Achilles tendon at the first sign of trouble, it most likely won't progress to this level of damage.)

RECOVERING

Don't start running again until you can do toe raises without pain. Instead, cycle in low gears, swim, or run in a pool. Ice the area three to four times a day if possible, for 20 minutes at a time. When the tendon is less tender, gradually resume your training load and intensity. Avoid hills, track workouts, and longer runs.

PREVENTING

• Keep your Achilles tendon flexible. Stretch by standing on the balls of your feet on a raised surface such as a stair or a curb. Drop your heels down and hold for a 10-count.
• Do calf stretching exercises (see page 25–27).
• Do hamstring stretching exercises (see page 29).
• Choose motion control shoes designed for overpronators.
• Choose shoes with a heel cup that supports your heel and keeps your tendon from over stretching.
• Replace your worn out shoes.
• Schedule an evaluation by a podiatrist to see if you need orthotics.
• Decrease hill training, speed workouts, and track workouts.
• Make gradual increases in your training.
• Ice the injury as needed.

Heel Bruise

A heel bruise is one of many types of heel pain. A heel bruise can be caused by a single incident (for example, stepping barefoot on a rock, or awkwardly stepping on a sharp object while running), or it can be a chronic injury. Older runners may be more prone to heel bruises, because the thickness of the heel pad decreases with age.

RECOGNIZING

The pain usually is in the middle of the heel, which is quite tender to the touch. The heel tends to be sorer upon waking or after sitting for a long time. But, unlike a low-level Achilles tendonitis injury, the pain doesn't wear off, partly because you put pressure on the bruise with each step taken.

TREATING

Insert a heel cushion to provide cushioning and absorb shock. Cushions have a soft point in the middle (creating a doughnut effect) that protects the heel bruise. Control inflammation with ice and an anti-inflammatory such as ibuprofen or aspirin.

RECOVERING

Unless the bruise is too severe, you should be able to continue running with the heel cushion. Monitor the bruise, and if it gets worse during your runs, cut back on your running. Instead, cross train by doing something that isn't weight-bearing (swimming, cycling, and so on).

PREVENTING

If you are predisposed to heel injuries you can place extra cushioning in your shoe as a pre-ventative measure rather that an after-the-fact treatment.

• In general, maintaining a healthy weight can certainly help cut down on the occurrence of heel bruising.

• Since most of these injuries are caused by landing on stray materials in your path, your best safeguard is to keep your eyes open and try to avoid rocky patches.

• Wearing thicker socks or an extra pair can absorb some additional shock.

Other than that, there's not much you can do here except not running barefoot and steering clear of rough terrain.

Plantar Fasciitis

The plantar fascia is a band of fibrous tissue that runs from under the heel to the base of your toes and supports your arch. If this band is short, you will have high arches; if it's long, you will have low arches. The more you overpronate, the more you stress your fascia. Because the fascia isn't very flexible, it tears. The tears heal with scar tissue, which is even more inflexible than the fascia, and more tearing results.

A tight Achilles tendon can also put considerable stress on the plantar fascia, and weight gain can make the problem worse. Other contributing factors are sudden increases in training mileage, beginning speed work, or switching surfaces (particularly to concrete sidewalks). Those who wear high heels all day and then switch into flat running shoes are also at risk.

RECOGNIZING

You'll feel deep and intense pain at the base of your heel, almost like a bruise. You can also feel pain along the bottom of the arch, where the fascia feels stretched and taut (this pain is more pronounced when you flex your toes). The pain is worse upon rising and after you've been sitting for a while. It subsides as you move

Hard surfaces such as concrete should be avoided when coping with aggravated plantar fascia.

around, because the fascia lengthens slightly as you move. It can be especially painful during or after your run.

TREATING

Cut back on your running. Take an anti-inflammatory such as ibuprofen or aspirin, and ice the area for 20 minutes several times a day. A great way to do this is with a paper cup that you've frozen water in. Peel off part of the paper cup and roll your foot over it, from your heel to the ball of your foot and back.

Do Achilles tendon stretches first thing in the morning. Try to do this stretch while you're still lying in bed: Loop a towel around the bottom of your foot and pull your toes toward your nose for 30 seconds, relax, and repeat twice. During the day, do wall pushups with straight legs for one set, then with bent legs. It's best to do the pushups barefoot.

If you haven't recovered within four weeks, see a doctor.

RECOVERING

For mild cases, cut back on mileage, and avoid hills and speed work. Consider seeing a podiatrist to see if you need orthotics or if your current orthotics need to be replaced. Cross train by swimming, running in a pool, and cycling in low gear.

For more severe cases, you may need to take anywhere from four to eight weeks off from running. Your doctor might recommend a walking cast or night splints. A night splint keeps your foot flexed while you sleep (and thus keeps the calf stretched). Or your doctor might recommend that you have corticosteroids injected into the inflamed area to reduce the inflammation.

PREVENTING

• Choose shoes that help control your pronation, and replace before the heels have become significantly worn.
• Wear a heel cup or heel cushion in both running and regular shoes.
• Run on soft surfaces.
• Ice the affected area for 20 minutes after running.
• Avoid hill running.
• When beginning speed work, ease into it gradually with a several-week buildup.
• Stretch your plantar fascia: With your knee bent and ankle flexed, pull your toes back toward your ankle and hold for 10 seconds. Repeat 10 times a day.

Plantar Warts

Plantar warts, small growths on the sole of your foot caused by a virus, are a nuisance. The skin in these areas receives more pressure and is more likely to have a small crack that can be infiltrated by a virus.

Plantar warts can be contracted by walking barefoot in public swimming pools and locker rooms.

RECOGNIZING

Unlike common warts, plantar warts don't rise above the surface of the skin. You'll likely feel an uncomfortable spot where the wart is—sometimes as if you have a small stone in your shoe. With your foot under a bright light, look for brownish-black specks. Sand the growth down with sandpaper or a pumice stone and reinspect it. If you see brown specks, it's probably a plantar wart.

TREATING

To kill the wart, apply an over-the-counter salicylic acid preparation, available in liquid, gel, pad, or ointment. Periodically sand and retreat the wart. It can take several months to get rid of a large one. Warts can spread, so monitor your feet closely and treat warts early.

Another option is to apply vitamin A once a day by breaking open a capsule and squeezing the liquid onto the wart. It can take anywhere from one to nine months for warts to disappear using this method.

Other methods used to get rid of warts include excision, freezing, burning, acids, and laser treatment. Consult your doctor.

RECOVERING

For temporary relief of pain, place a doughnut-shaped piece of molefoam around the wart. Continue to run if it's not too painful.

PREVENTING

• Keep your feet as dry as possible.
• Wear socks made of synthetic material. Change them regularly.
• Use medicated foot powder.
• Don't go barefoot in locker rooms or public showers. Invest in an inexpensive pair of flip flops or shower shoes.

A THICK-SKINNED RUNNER

The friction and pressure of running can produce thickened skin on your feet, which forms to protect you. These areas of thickened skin are calluses, which are usually painless.

Calluses normally develop on the portions of the soles that bear the most weight. If pain does occur, use metatarsal pads on the callus and soft inserts in your shoes. After soaking your feet in warm water, you can file the callus with an emery board, sandpaper, or a pumice stone. Apply petroleum jelly or another moisturizer. For very thick, painful calluses, seek advice from a sports-oriented physician.

To prevent calluses, make sure your shoes fit well and keep your feet moisturized; dry feet are more susceptible to friction.

Blisters

Compared to more serious injuries, blisters can seem frivolous. But they can be painful. Blisters are caused by friction, usually your shoes or socks rubbing against your skin. In response to the friction, the body produces fluid, which builds up under the skin being rubbed. A blood blister occurs when the friction ruptures tiny blood vessels. Blisters are more likely to happen in hot or wet weather, which makes your feet swell and intensifies friction.

RECOGNIZING

Blisters are puffed-up sacs of skin, bulging with the liquid that developed when the friction began. A blood blister is just that: a blister filled with blood, rather than clear fluid.

TREATING

The majority of blisters will simply recede on their own, the fluid will be reabsorbed, and your skin will easily heal. For the most part, if you remain patient with this injury, you'll be just fine.

A good pair of socks will help cut down the friction between your foot and shoe which can cause blisters.

If a larger blister hasn't subsided in 24 hours and is troublesome, you may want to drain it. (Do not, however, drain a blood blister.) Here's how:

1. Wash your hands.
2. Sterilize a needle in a flame, in boiling water, or by soaking it in rubbing alcohol.
3. Swab the blister with alcohol or disinfectant.
4. Carefully prick two small holes in the blister, on opposite sides, just deeply enough to open the dead skin.
5. Gently push on the outer edges of the blister with sterile gauze. Take care not to push on the part that you punctured.
6. Cover the blister with a sterile bandage. Keep wearing a bandage until the skin toughens up.

RECOVERING

Blisters are one of the most common and non-threatening injuries a runner can incur but it doesn't mean you should laugh them off completely. As with just about any other skin wound, blisters should improve with each passing day so long as you're not irritating them further. But if pain, redness, and swelling persist, you may be dealing with an infection. See your physician for further treatment.

If, however, your blister is cleaned, treated and healing normally you may feel free to restart your running routine. Before you lace up your shoes and get back out there, try the following tip.

Before running, cut a doughnut shape out of molefoam and place around the blister, then place another layer of molefoam on top of the entire area.

PREVENTING

• Wear synthetic socks, which wick moisture away from the skin. Socks with reinforced heels and toes also help reduce friction.
• Dry skin is also prone to friction, so use skin moisturizers.
• Coat your feet with Vaseline or another lubricant before you run. Just don't get carried away—a little goes a long way.
• Wear shoes that fit. Too big and your feet will slosh around in them; too small and your toes will rub against the front of the shoes.
• Use padded tape, which stays put when your feet get wet, and protects your feet against friction.
• Wear two pairs of socks, so the friction occurs between the socks, and not the feet and socks. (You may need to switch to slightly larger shoes to accommodate the extra socks.)

Athlete's Foot

Athlete's foot is a fungal infection of the foot. Your body (whether you knew it or not) is home to many micro-organisms, including fungi. When a particular type of fungus grows and spreads on your feet you get *tinea pedis*, which is commonly known as athlete's foot.

RECOGNIZING

Athlete's foot results in itchy, red, flaking, and sometimes cracked skin, often between the toes. More severe cases might cause blisters or oozing of fluids.

TREATING

Many over-the-counter treatments can be effective in fighting athlete's foot. These creams or powders contain clotrimazole, tolnaflate, or miconazole. You usually have to use these medicines for one to two weeks before the fungus is cleared.

If your athlete's foot doesn't respond to such treatment within two to four weeks, or if it continually reoccurs, see your doctor for a stronger antifungal medication. A prescription may be a better bet.

Athlete's foot is generally harmless and easy to take care of, but you should call your doctor right away if your foot is swollen, warm, and has red streaks, or if you have diabetes.

RECOVERING

While recovering from athlete's foot, consistently apply the medication you are using, and keep your feet clean and dry, especially between the toes. When you wash your feet, wash them thoroughly between the toes. Change your socks often to keep your feet as dry as possible. To relieve the itching, soak your feet in baking soda mixed with water.

Keeping your feet dry and well ventilated are two ways to combat athlete's foot.

PREVENTING

• Fungi like moisture, so dry your feet thoroughly after bathing or swimming.

• Don't hang out in your wet socks after running; shower and change into dry socks.

• Wash your feet thoroughly.

• Use antifungal foot powder, especially if you will be in a locker room or public shower.

• Don't go barefoot in locker rooms or public showers.

• Wear light shoes with plenty of ventilation or "air holes" which will allow your feet to breathe.

A FEW WORDS ON BUNIONS

The foot injury with the odd name, a bunion is caused by a build up of bone or hard tissue on and around the joint at the base of the big toe. This condition can force the big toe to bend in and overlap with other toes giving the foot a strange angular look. Bunions can be the result of anything from a genetic predisposition towards flat feet to ill-fitting shoes to poor foot mechanics

On top of the ugly appearance, some bunions can be quite painful. While the severity varies, this is one of those conditions that can progress from minor swelling and discomfort to something much more debilitating. Many athletes are discouraged from having bunion surgery due to the fact that it can limit the motion in the big toe, others have no choice but to undergo the procedure that shaves down the bump and realigns the big toe. It can take up to two months for your foot to fully heal.

Many bunions are unavoidable, but there are still some preventative measures you can take to decrease your chances.

• Stay away from shoes with a cramped toebox. Women's shoes can be especially guilty of this offense.

• Use bunion pads (available at any phramacy) to ease the friction in your shoe.

• Get orthotics to help your feet from overpronation.

• Give your feet a breather during the day by removing your shoes.

Try not to get too discouraged. You're not the only one living with bunions.

Ankle Injuries

Even the most experienced of runners fall victim to ankle sprains from time to time.

Ankle sprains are the most common ankle injury. They occur when your foot accidentally rolls to the outside, stretching or tearing the ankle ligaments and causing an inversion sprain or strain. If the ankle rolls to the inside, it's called an eversion sprain (this is much less common).

RECOGNIZING

You'll feel sharp pain and, almost immediately, experience swelling. A Grade I sprain involves stretching or minor tearing of the ligament, while a Grade II sprain involves tearing or partial tearing of one or more of the ligaments.

A Grade III sprain means a complete tear of all three ligaments, and almost always requires surgery.

TREATING

For Grade I and Grade II sprains, the basic treatment is Rest, Ice, Compression, Elevation (RICE)—

and the sooner you do this, the less pain and swelling you'll have. (A Grade III sprain requires a visit to the doctor.)

Rest – Put little or no weight on your ankle for at least the first 24 hours after the injury. Use crutches for a severe sprain.

Ice – Ice the ankle every two or three hours for 20 minutes at a time for the first 72 hours. Use ice packs, ice slush baths, or ice massages (using a cup with frozen water; rub the ice over the sprained portion, continue to move it around).

Compression – Wrap your ankle with an elastic wrap to help keep the swelling down. Wrap it tightly but not so much that it cuts off your circulation.

Elevation – Keep your ankle raised above heart level to reduce the swelling.

Avoid aspirin, which can cause more bleeding into the ankle; use ibuprofen or acetaminophen instead.

RECOVERING

As your ankle mends, you can gradually progress to more and more weight bearing. You may support your ankle with a brace or tape it with wide, nonelastic adhesive tape until it regains strength.

As soon as you have enough strength, do non-weight-bearing stretching and strengthening exercises, such as drawing the letters of the alphabet with your toes.

Most ankle sprains heal within a few weeks. The more severe the injury, the longer the recovery.

PREVENTING

- Do towel exercise (see page 76).
- Do band exercises (see page 34).
- Do alphabet exercise: Use your big toe to "write" the alphabet in the air, moving your ankle to form the letter, and repeat three times.

Ice and elevate your ankle as soon as possible after you've injured it.

Listen Up!

We know that sometimes you are tempted to ignore your symptoms and carry on running. Of course you can injure yourself that way, and we hope you pay attention to all your symptoms. There are nine symptoms, however, you should never, ever ignore.

Chest pressure. Chest pressure, often described as a fullness or tightness, could be a sign of coronary heart disease or a heart attack in progress. The discomfort often radiates to the arms, neck, and jaw, and it doesn't have to last long to signify something serious. Get checked out immediately by a doctor or, better yet, a cardiologist.

Lightheadedness and irregular heartbeat. These may indicate a rhythm disturbance or a congenital heart defect called hypertrophic myopathy. The lightheadedness or irregular heartbeat can occur during or up to two hours after exercise. See a cardiologist.

Unusual fatigue. If you become easily winded or exhausted during a normal training run—especially if this happens several days in a row—don't just assume there's something wrong with your training. Ongoing fatigue may signify heart problems, exercise-induced asthma, Lyme disease, diabetes, chronic fatigue syndrome, or another malady. Cut your mileage in half for a week, and avoid any hard workouts. If you still feel fatigue at the end of a week, see your doctor.

Localized bone pain. Shinsplints cause pain over a broad area, but pinpointed pain may mean a stress fracture. Ignore this, and the stress fracture can become a complete break, meaning more time healing and no time running. If your shin pain is localized, see a podiatrist or orthopedist.

Lumps and bumps on the lower leg. Runners suffer from two common types of lumpy masses: small nodules on the Achilles tendon and lumps on the side of the knee. A nodule on the tendon implies tendonosis, a degeneration of the tendon, which causes scar tissue. Treatment usually involves physical therapy and rest. Lumps or cysts on the side of the knee normally form in relation to meniscus tears. In these cases, treatment consists of repairing the meniscus and letting the cyst dissolve on its own. See an orthopedist if you feel these lumps.

Disorientation, nausea, or stopping sweating during warm-weather running. These symptoms can indicate heat stroke, which can be fatal. Stop exercising, find some shade (preferably an air-conditioned building or car) and drink plenty of fluids. If the symptoms persist for more than a few minutes, get to an emergency room for intravenous fluids.

Headache during running. Some headaches that come on during exercise can be quite harmless, but others can signify a life-threatening illness such as a leaking brain aneurysm or coronary artery blockage. Often these headaches feel like migraines, and they include nausea and sensitivity to light. Stop running until you see your doctor.

Cold and flu symptoms. A case of the sniffles shouldn't stop you from running. But watch out for fever, deep body aches, and malaise, which are signs of a more serious viral infection. Don't exercise when you have a virus, especially when you have a fever. If your symptoms are all above the neck, chances are it's a cold, and you can go for an easy run. But if your symptoms are below the neck, such as chills and body aches, you probably have the flu, and should not run.

Amenorrhea. Women who train intensely—and who don't eat enough to keep up with the demands of that training—may stop having their menstrual periods. The estrogen deficiency that causes amenorrhea also can cause bone loss and osteoporosis. It's not heavy training that causes amenorrhea, but not getting enough calories to support the rigors of that training. See your physician, a sports gynecologist, or a nutritionist.

Listen to your body and don't ignore symptoms.

PART IV:
DEALING WITH INJURY

Coping Physically

First things first. An injury is physical, and you have to deal with its physical aspects, so you'll recover quickly and come back as healthy as possible. Here's how.

Troubleshoot. It's important to know why your injury occurred in the first place. Look through your training log; consider the shape of your shoes. Were you running too much? Too fast? Neglecting to cross train? Reshape your training plan to avoid another such injury. If you just treat the symptoms, and not the cause, you'll be more likely to keep getting the same injury again and again.

See a sports medicine professional. If you aren't sure how to treat your injury yourself, or if it's beyond the self-treatment stage, seek out a sports-oriented doctor. Ask questions; take notes.

Maintain your fitness. This is the good news: You can maintain most, if not all, of your fitness when you are injured. If you can run a little, do so carefully, and take up the slack with cross training. Otherwise, approximate your training load as closely as you can with cross training.

Build your strength and flexibility. You have to be careful here, because you don't want to make your injury worse. But there are many ways you can build strength and flexibility while you are injured—and doing so will not only hasten your comeback, but also lessen your chances of incurring the same injury. You'll find exercises in Part II, with some additional ones under specific ailments in Part III.

Keep it vigorous. If you normally run 45 minutes a day, do some activity vigorous enough to keep you aerobic for 45 minutes a day. This is critical for hanging on to your sanity, not to mention your aerobic fitness. It doesn't matter much what you do as long as it doesn't aggravate the existing injury. Several studies suggest that if you do aerobic alternatives properly and with high enough intensity, they can maintain and even increase your fitness level during your time off.

Swimming is a fantastic way to stay in shape while recovering from an injury.

Maintain your health. Don't lapse into an unhealthy lifestyle: lying around, eating poorly, gaining weight. It will make your recovery tougher, and you'll be miserable when you do return to running.

Even if you're not ready to take on aerobic or strength training, you should be mobile enough to get up and go out for a walk. Since you've been a little more sedentary than usual the best place to start is with a trip to your local market for some healthy snacks and food to counterbalance your lack of activity.

Making yourself homemade meals with high protein, low-fat ingredients such as chicken and fish can help transform your body in ways exercise can't. Substituting fresh fruits and vegetables for those salty snacks will go a long way to keeping you healthy.

Overall, you should look at this downtime as an educational experience. When you are fully recovered and running again you will have a better understanding of your body and be well equipped to recognize and avoid potential injury pitfalls.

Coping Mentally

Let's face it, a running injury can be quite depressing. For many of us, running provides a sense of our self-identity, improves our self-esteem, and helps us cope with the daily stresses of life. When you can't run, it can be easy to get depressed. But your mental attitude and approach will significantly affect your rehabilitation. An optimistic approach will help you get back on the road much faster. Here's how to smooth your road to recovery.

Map out your rehabilitation plan. Plan what you need to do to recover and set about doing it. Set realistic rehab goals. Readjust your running goals.

Stick to your routine. You may not be able to run on your lunch hour, but do whatever form of physical activity your injury will allow at the same time you normally run. Following rituals will help lift your mood, and it will be easy to slide back into running when you're able.

Stay connected. Stay in touch with your running friends; you can volunteer at races or go to club meetings. Read some running magazines and keep up with the sport. Spend time with your family and with other friends as well. Basically, keep yourself involved in running any way you can.

Do something daily. Every day, without fail, do something that helps you heal. This may be icing your injured area, doing a stretch, or using a rowing machine. Taking action will both speed your recovery and help you maintain peace of mind.

Realize you're more than a runner. You may love running. It may be one of the most joyful parts of your day and your life. You may socialize with lots of other runners. Your bookshelves may be filled with running books. You may go from race to race almost every weekend. But you're more than a runner. Spend time doing your other activities and interests.

Find ways to cope with stress. Yes, running is a great way to relieve stress, but there are other ways. Cross training should help

Don't forget your friends on your road to recovery.

Share your plan. If someone knows you're rehabbing a strained hamstring, that person might be able to give you some good exercises—or some words of encouragement. And you might find yourself in a position to mentor or coach some other runner through an injury. This makes you feel valued and useful, still connected to the sport, to your friends, and to your plan. You are being proactive and positive.

Think of your layoff as part of your training. It's what you need to do at the moment to continue your training. Keep focused on the rehabilitation exercises you need to do to get back to running.

Treat yourself. Now's the time for a new pair of running shoes or the running clothes you've been wanting. They'll be ready for you when you are ready to run again.

Keep it in perspective. You're not dead. An Achilles tendon injury isn't a diagnosis of a terminal illness. Count your blessings. You simply took a slight detour. You'll be back in a relatively short time. In the meantime, explore new activities, maintain your fitness, and keep on enjoying life.

you relieve your stress, but also find other activities to take part in: for example, woodworking, painting, a new hobby, volunteering your time and helping someone else.

Think positively. Your mental attitude is critical to your recovery. You're along for the ride; you might as well enjoy it—and speed it up a bit by being proactive towards your own recovery.

Sample Training Diary

As we mentioned earlier in the book (see pages 12–13) keeping a training diary is a great way to track your progress and monitor areas of your training where you may need help. There are any number of runner's diaries available to you in bookstores or you can buy a notebook and simply make your own. Below we offer what a sample diary page might look like. There are certain elements such as distance and time which you'll find in every diary but you need not limit yourself as to what you record. It's your diary, tailor it to your specific needs.

SAMPLE DIARY PAGE

Date: **August 14**

Route: **Savoy Road**

Distance: **6 miles**
Time: **41:12**
Pace: **6:52/mile**
Weather: **82 F (27.7 C), not humid**

Notes: **Felt strong last 3 miles. Pace was controlled.**

Resting heart rate: **48 beats per minute**
Training heart rate: **136 beats per minute**

Goals for week: **40 miles**

Weekly mileage: **22 miles**

Monthly mileage: **81 miles**

Return to Running

You're on your way back! You've begun training again. You're overjoyed, but a little wary about injuring yourself again. (And it's good to be a little wary.) Remember these guidelines as you're coming back from injury.

Stretch and strengthen. This is what your rehab is all about. It's crucial to recovery, and to staying injury-free. Follow the programs in Part II. Don't push yourself too far too fast too soon but don't be afraid either. You'll get a feel for how much you can do.

Continue to cross train. Keep up your cross training as you continue to regain strength in the injured area. Err on the side of caution here; it's better to lightly test your recently recovered hamstring or Achilles tendon on the road and supplement that training on a bike or in a pool than to injure yourself again. If you are concerned about an impact-related injury there are numerous machines at your local gym, such as elliptical trainers, which will give you a great workout wihout the pounding on your bones and joints.

Listen to your body. Of course we had to end with this. This should underlay everything you do in your approach to your training, your recognition and treatment of injury, your rehabilitation and recovery from injury, and—next time around—your prevention of a potential injury. You now have all the knowledge at your fingertips. May all your runs from here on out be injury free!

Understanding injuries will keep you on track for a healthy and successful running regimen.

INDEX

Numbers in **bold** refer to pages with illustrations

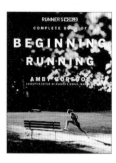
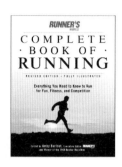
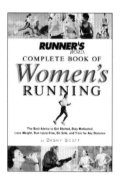